NOW WHAT DO I DO?

SETTLING YOUR SPOUSE'S ESTATE
ORGANIZING AND SIMPLIFYING THE PROCESS

By

Teresa M. O'Brien

NOW WHAT DO I DO?

SETTLING YOUR SPOUSE'S ESTATE
ORGANIZING AND SIMPLIFYING THE PROCESS

Disclaimer: While helpful hints and reminders are provided throughout the book for completing the tables, they are in no way to be considered a substitute for legal and financial counsel. Please check with all the members of your professional team for the latest legal requirements and processes. O'Brien Consulting Group, LLC., assumes no responsibility for legal or financial processes.

Copyright © 2020 Teresa M. O'Brien

ISBN: 9780979157769

All Rights Reserved

Table of Contents

HOW TO USE THIS WORKBOOK 1

FUNERAL PREPARATIONS 3

FUNERAL ARRANGEMENTS 5

PAYING FOR THE FUNERAL 7

FAMILY AND FRIENDS TO HELP ME 9

GETTING STARTED 11
    KEY DAILY CONTACTS 12
    GATHERING DOCUMENTS 16
    DOCUMENT TRAVEL BAG 17
    MY OWN CURRENT INCOME SOURCES 20
    MY SPOUSE'S INCOME AT TIME OF DEATH 22
    OBTAINING OTHER SURVIVOR BENEFITS 26
    NOW WHAT WILL MY NEW INCOME BE? 27

FINANCIAL ASSETS 29
    BANK ACCOUNTS 30
    INVESTMENT ACCOUNTS 33
    QUALIFIED RETIREMENT PLANS 37
    INSURANCE POLICIES I INTEND TO KEEP 40
    NON-FINANCIAL ASSETS 41
    WHO ARE THE NEW BENEFICIARIES? 42
    SUMMARY OF ASSETS AND COST BASIS 44

LIABILITIES: MORTGAGES, LOANS, AND NOTES 47

DEBTS AND BILLS: MAINTAIN, REDUCE, OR ELIMINATE? 49
    NOW WHAT BILLS CAN I CANCEL? 58
    BILLS I WANT TO REDUCE 62
    EXPENSES I WANT TO KEEP AT CURRENT LEVEL 66
    NEW HOUSEHOLD MONTHLY EXPENSES SUMMARY 70

SOCIAL MEDIA / OTHER ONLINE ACCOUNTS 73

SUMMARY SECTION 75
    NET WORTH SUMMARY 76
    MONTHLY BUDGET 77

HOW TO USE THIS WORKBOOK

My heart goes out to you as you attempt to move forward. Losing a spouse is devastating. After my sister's husband died in 2018 and, even though she had been actively involved in their finances, I noticed how she still struggled getting started with the mountain of details and paperwork she faced. Yes, she found suggestions in other books as well as with her lawyer and her accountant, of what to do and categories of things to do, but there appeared no organized way of handling the information needed to put her financial life back together. I then walked her through what I had done to handle our parents' estate after our mother's death, and she found what I had outlined very helpful. This is how the idea for this workbook was created.

Once my sister had an organized way to approach the task and had developed a method to track her progress, she was on her way. She realized that many of her married friends were not as actively involved in their family finances and would likely have an even harder time knowing how to work through everything. So, she suggested I write a book that would make it easier for recent widow(er)s to get organized and move forward.

There are excellent local widow and widower support groups (clergy, widow and widower groups, psychiatrists and psychologists, friends, and family members) who provide emotional support as you go through the stages of grief (denial, anger, bargaining, depression, and acceptance). There are also many excellent executor and trustee books on what must be done, through whom, and caveats on the process. But the actual tables you will need to organize your information are usually left up to you to create.

This workbook is a combination of the learnings my sister and I developed as we handled our responsibilities as executors and trustees. It can be used with any book or professional whose advice you are following. It is written in the general timeline of when you will be doing things. It can also be used as a guide for settling any estate or as a 'conversation starter guide' for pre-planning.

This book provides an easy and focused way to follow and note your progress while addressing the necessary changes to your finances at a time when you may feel scattered, distracted, and overwhelmed. This book is designed to help you review your current financial life and decide what is best for you to do (or not do) for your future financial life. **It _doesn't_** automatically mean that you **have** to change **_everything_**.

Since the process of settling the estate can take months, and some cases years, to complete, this is a workbook to help you track what is completed and what still is in progress. This book is meant to be used as a guide to help organize and simplify the process, so write on the pages, add sticky notes, highlight lines, whatever you find helpful. For those items that are incomplete, you can note what actions are being taken by whom. When everything is done, keep the book as a reminder of how accounts currently stand. Even if someone else is helping you through the process, you can still use this book to track their progress and maintain a log of how your accounts are now arranged.

NOTE: <u>Keep copies of everything that you send by US Postal mail. Copy yourself on every email that you send.</u> Not only will this help you remember what you have sent, but if the recipient fails to get what you sent, you can quickly resend the information. It also makes it easy to jointly discuss any follow-up over the phone.

You may often find that you start each contact with a new company by leaving messages. Therefore, spend a few minutes writing down bullet points for why you are calling so you can leave a short message. Always give your name, your spouse's legal name, and your call back number twice in the call – once at the beginning and once at the end. Having all that information at the very beginning of the call makes it easier for them to re-listen to the call for any of it that they missed. Having it at the end gives them a second chance to get all of it the first time through the message. When you do reach someone, always ask for a direct line number for any further callbacks and in case you get disconnected.

Be patient with yourself and others, but be persistent. Get a commitment for a date when the required action will likely be completed and get a call back number for follow-up to use when that date arrives. Always get the name of the person you are speaking with. People tend to take a little extra care when they know you care enough about them to find out something as simple as their name.

FUNERAL PREPARATIONS

If you still need funeral planning, here are some helpful guides.

Most funeral homes will coordinate the initial purchase of death certificates. Although everyone's situation is different, 10-15 should be sufficient since many places will return the original copy after they have made a copy for their files (especially if accounts are local). Some businesses will accept receipt of death certificates via fax or email.

Funeral homes are the most efficient way to get these certificates. They may even issue a temporary one for you.

Most funeral homes will notify Social Security and Veterans Affairs of your spouse's death, but it pays to follow up to verify notification has taken place.

FUNERAL ARRANGEMENTS

Funeral homes will talk you through the funeral arrangements, but it is good to take notes and write down any agreements or follow-up questions. Some funeral homes will give you support resources when you use their services. Sort through these resources to find any that will help you and begin using them immediately. If you and your spouse had previously discussed your spouse's funeral wishes, bring those with you to the meeting with the funeral director. Life insurance or pre-paid funeral/burial policies may cover some or all of these expenses.

Item	Notes
Spouse's written instructions for funeral arrangements	
My funeral/burial budget	
Funeral home's options pricing	
Funeral home's payment terms	
Items to be buried with spouse	
Visitation hours	
Funeral service hours	
Interment/Inurnment hours	
Funeral home hours for drop off/pickup of items	
Burial plot deed	
Cremation	

Item	Notes
Columbarium Niche	
Memorial Service - **Funeral Observances** - **Pallbearers** - **Eulogies** - **Music**	
Disposition of ashes	
Transportation	
Post funeral gathering	
Food	
Obituary	
Flowers	
Charities for donations & fund distribution	
Prepaid thank you cards	
Social Security and VA notifications	
Death Certificates (10-15 certified copies)	

PAYING FOR THE FUNERAL

Where is all the money coming from to pay for the funeral? Typical sources of available funds in the first 30 days are **pre-paid funeral/burial policies, cash, checking accounts, money market accounts, savings accounts, CDs, credit cards, and brokerage accounts**. Focus here first if your funeral home requires up-front payment for their services (which many funeral homes do.)

You will be looking for **accounts that the survivor has access to**. If only your spouse had access to the account, that account could be frozen. The account may not be able to be used until the official release of funds after notification of your spouse's death by the trustee or executor.

After meeting with the funeral director, your immediate cash requirement for funeral expenses is $_____.

SOURCES OF MONEY TO PAY FOR THE FUNERAL

Source	Account Number	Available Money	Online UserID	Online Password	Who Has Authorized Access?

FAMILY AND FRIENDS TO HELP ME

With so many questions and needs coming at you all at once, use your mental energy where it will do you the most good. Delegate as much to others (family, friends, and business colleagues) as possible – especially at the beginning – so that you can stay focused on those things that only YOU, THE SURVIVING SPOUSE, MUST DO.

Activity	Person Responsible	Contact Information	Responsibility Assigned
Updating family (keep list with contact info)			
Updating friends (keep list with contact info)			
Updating co-workers (ask someone from work)			
Watching minor children			
Cancelling spouse's appointments			
Watching pets			

GETTING STARTED

Over the first several weeks and months, there will be people and organizations that you will be contacting multiple times. The following tables can be used to note their contact information or you can put the information into your smart phone.

KEY DAILY CONTACTS

Type	Contact Name	Phone	Email	Fax
Funeral Home				
Cemetery				
Social Security				
Spouse's Current Employer				
Spouse's Former Employer 1				
Spouse's Former Employer 2				
Medicare				
Medicaid				
Veterans Affairs				

PROFESSIONAL TEAM MEMBERS

Type	Contact Name	Phone	Email	Fax
Family Lawyer				
Business Lawyer				
Accountant				
Financial Planner				
Insurance Rep				

DISCUSSION WITH AN ATTORNEY: EXECUTING WILL OR TRUST DIRECTIVES

These documents indicate who will be the trustee of your spouse's trust and the executor of your spouse's will. If you are not the named individual, then verify the acceptance of the responsibilities by those named in these documents.

Review the will and trust documents immediately, in case there is any information that needs immediate attention. Prioritize the rest and complete in a timely manner.

Because every state has different legal requirements, it is best to consult with your attorney for guidance about any questions pertaining to these legal documents, such as:

- Will or trust execution process (including certified letters of appointment for personal representative or Letters of Testamentary)
- Filing of will in probate court (if needed)
- Notification of creditors
- Liability for deceased spouse's debts and priority of claims
- Handling transition of your spouse's business ownership (if applicable)
- Costs and fees to attorney
- Preparing list of deceased spouse's personal, non-financial assets (i.e. jewelry, boats, etc.), along with their approximate value
- Annual estate accounting procedure/paperwork
- Whom to contact when you have follow-up questions and that person's contact information
- Preparing revised will or trust documents

DISCUSSION WITH AN ACCOUNTANT: TAXES, COST BASIS, & BUDGET

Accountants can help you understand how to organize your key financial documents to make it easier for them to help you with preparing your taxes and assessing the status of your finances going forward. Some initial topics to cover with your accountant:

- What information accountant needs from you to determine which taxes need filing (both at state and federal level) and by what date
- Required EIN number
- Knowledge of rules of spousal transfer of funds from retirement accounts (IRAs, 401K, 403B, SEPs, SIMPLEs, etc.) to minimize negative tax consequences
- What records to keep and for how long
- How to determine cost basis of assets, where required
- Tips on creating a budget
- What fees will be charged by the accountant
- Whom to contact at accountant's office for any follow-up questions and that person's contact information

GATHERING DOCUMENTS

As you begin updating and handling your legal and financial affairs, there are documents that you will need to take with you to almost every meeting or have available for any phone calls. They are listed in the first table below. The second table lists items that may be needed, depending upon the specific meeting. It is good to collect them all in **one convenient location**. Check off each item as you find it. For those items you don't put into this one place, note the item's current location next to the item in the table below. Reminder: Death Certificates can be applied for through the funeral home that handled your spouse's services.

MOST OFTEN NEEDED DOCUMENTS

☐ Will	☐ Marriage license
☐ Trust	☐ Spouse's death certificate
☐ Spouse's birth certificate	☐ Military discharge papers
☐ Adoption papers	☐ Passport or citizenship papers
☐ Spouse's Social Security card	☐ Your Social Security card
☐ Divorce agreement/decree	☐ Birth certificates of minor children
☐ Naturalization papers	☐ List of user names & passwords

DOCUMENTS YOU MAY ALSO NEED

☐ Life insurance policy numbers	☐ Rental property leases	☐ Safe deposit box number and key
☐ Spouse's employee/retiree number(s)	☐ Deeds	☐ Storage locker contract and key
☐ Spouse's Medicare number	☐ Loan statements (recent)	☐ Annuity contract numbers
☐ Tax returns (last 2 years)	☐ Motor vehicle titles	☐ Employee benefits information
☐ Bank statements (recent)	☐ Car insurance	☐ Military service records
☐ Mortgage statements (recent)	☐ Homeowner's insurance	☐ Record of assets
☐ Investment account statements (recent)	☐ Health insurance	☐ Business ownership/interest documents
☐ Post Office box agreement & key	☐ Prenuptial agreement	☐ Postnuptial agreement
☐ Credit card list	☐ Car lease agreement	☐ Airline mileage numbers
☐	☐ Voter registration card	☐

DOCUMENT TRAVEL BAG

Get a distinctive cloth bag or portfolio that can contain:

- favorite picture of your spouse
- all the relevant items in the "Most Often Needed Documents" above
- notebook to keep track of tasks and other notes or a 3-ring binder
- pens, paper/binder clips, a Post It© notepad, and a highlighter
- a "reminder" calendar for key dates & follow-up, an easy to use calculator
- any meeting specific paperwork or any paperwork given to you at each meeting
- this book – it was made to be marked up – feel free

Always put this document travel bag back in the EXACT SAME location when you return home. You never want to have to search for the location of your document travel bag. People will return your calls at random times with follow-up questions so easy access to your document travel bag is essential at all times. These are difficult times and it is helpful to find ways to simplify your life and reduce undue stress. This is one way to do so. It is best to keep your bag in a workspace area where you will likely be handling the papers (a desk or an office).

A file drawer would be useful for storing completed paperwork. The following file folders should get you started: Utilities, Tax Statements, Loans/Leases, Credit Cards, Bank Statements, Brokerage Statements, Insurance, Medical Expenses, Employment, Death Certificates, Funeral. You can then adjust as you go.

Be prepared to take notes during every meeting or phone call. Highlight any action item that either you or the other person has agreed to complete. Include the date of the conversation and the name of person contacted. Make notations in this book as you receive new information or complete tasks.

Keep copies of everything that you send by US Postal mail. Copy yourself on every email that you send.

Not only will this help you remember what you have sent but if the recipient fails to get what you sent, you can quickly resend the information. It also makes it easy to jointly discuss any follow-up over the phone.

WHERE WILL MY MONEY COME FROM FOR THE NEXT FEW MONTHS?

Where is the money coming from to pay for your daily living expenses for the next 2-3 months?

These resources are likely to come from any money remaining in the above accounts after paying funeral expenses (summarized in tables on pages 30-39), plus any pension or salary checks earned in your own name, IRA distributions, and rental income. It could take a couple months before you receive any survivor income from your spouse's employer, government agency checks, or any proceeds from insurance policies that are cashed in. Your immediate income can be broken into four areas:

- your own current income,
- your surviving spouse income,
- survivor benefits from your spouse's death, and
- insurance policies that activated as a result of your spouse's death.

MY OWN CURRENT INCOME SOURCES

Type	Source	Contact Info	Current Amount	Future Amount
Salary				
Pension				
Social Security				
Veteran Affairs				
Alimony				
Stocks, Bonds, Mutual Funds				
Annuity				
401K				
403B				
Traditional IRA				
Roth IRA				

Type	Source	Contact Info	Current Amount	Future Amount
SEP				
SIMPLE				
Rental				
Royalty Fees				
TOTAL MONTHLY INCOME				

MY SPOUSE'S INCOME AT TIME OF DEATH

Because maintaining a continuous flow of income is so important, it is vital to get the death notifications to your spouse's income sources started as soon as possible. Determine which of your spouse's income sources existed at the time of death, notify the companies of the death, and determine survivor benefits, including payment terms (amount and timing). There may be multiple accounts for each type of income source.

Type	Institution	Account Number	Contact Person	Contact Information	Current Amount	Future Amount
Salary						
Pension						
Social Security						
Veterans Affairs						
Alimony						
Stocks, Bonds & Mutual Funds						
Annuity						
Life Insurance						
401 K						
403 B						

Type	Institution	Account Number	Contact Person	Contact Information	Current Amount	Future Amount
Traditional IRA						
Roth IRA						
SEP						
SIMPLE						
Rental						
Royalty Fees						
TOTAL MONTHLY INCOME						

TYPICAL TOPICS TO ASK MY SPOUSE'S EMPLOYER'S HUMAN RESOURCE (HR) DEPARTMENT

For most institutions, you will focus on only one or two areas of discussion for survivor benefits. But with an employer, there is not only the salary or pension to consider but the entire benefits package, including health benefits. Therefore, a special section for surviving spouse's questions has been included.

Use this list to get the conversation going with HR to make sure that you receive all the benefits to which you are entitled. After you have asked everything that you believe is relevant to your situation, please then ask, **"Are there any other payments or benefits that I didn't ask about that I should have for my situation?"** They are the experts at handling these situations. Let them guide you through the process.

- Accrued regular pay
- Accrued vacation or sick time pay
- Medical insurance options
- Pension and profit sharing plans
- Stock options
- Life insurance
- Qualified retirement account funds
- Flexible spending and HSA accounts
- Unreimbursed business or medical expenses
- COBRA insurance options for surviving spouse & dependent children
- Picking up spouse's personal effects from office
- Returning company's keys, badges, etc. to company

EMPLOYER AND GOVERNMENT SURVIVOR INCOME AND BENEFITS

Use this chart to summarize the information for both government and employer benefits.

Benefit	Amount	Start Date	Payout Amount	Payout Frequency	Termination Date

OBTAINING OTHER SURVIVOR BENEFITS

INSURANCE

Your spouse's death may have triggered the beginning of payout of some insurance, whether a lump sum payment or a continuous, ongoing payment, such as:

- Individual life insurance, group life insurance, employer based life insurance, accident/medical care insurance, long term care insurance, association sponsored insurance
- Credit life insurance for: credit card or bank sponsored insurance, mortgage insurance, union sponsored insurance, property insurance, travel insurance (See CREDIT LIFE INSURANCE TABLE on page 56).

Always **verify whether there is any part of a prepaid premium that can be returned to you**.

INSURANCE PAID TO ME

Company	Name on Policy	Policy Number	Death Benefit	Beneficiary	Payout Terms	Contact Name & Number

Those life insurance policies that you are not yet cashing in can be listed in the table on page 40.

NOW WHAT WILL MY NEW INCOME BE?

This next table is a quick visual for you to see your anticipated income sources and what to watch for until handling your finances becomes routine for you. While some of your income will be paid to you monthly, some may not.

For those that are paid on a quarterly basis, if you want to budget an amount each month, divide the amount that you receive each quarter by 3, then add that amount to this table. For those that are paid on an annual basis, if you want to budget an amount each month, divide the amount that you receive each year by 12, then add that amount to this table. Use the information found on pages 20-23, and 25 to complete this table.

Source	Monthly Amount	Payment Frequency	Date Paid	Comments
TOTAL:				

FINANCIAL ASSETS

This next section focuses on your household assets and the transition of these assets to the named beneficiaries.

Bank Accounts, Investment Accounts, and Retirement Accounts in your name can be used to cover any shortfall from your income stream in the first 60-90 days. Remember, this is about the time it will take for income from your spouse's survivor benefits to reach your bank account.

To make it easier for you to monitor your progress in settling the various accounts, separate tables have been created for each of these three areas (bank, investment, and retirement accounts) based on current ownership (spouse's name only, joint tenancy, or your name only). This will also make it easier for you to see which funds you can use immediately for living expenses.

BANK ACCOUNTS

BANK ACCOUNTS HELD IN SPOUSE'S NAME ONLY

Reminder: These funds will be available to you only after official release of the funds following proper notification of death by authorized executor or trustee.

Institution	Account Type & Number	Value	Ownership	Contact Information	Username	Password

BANK ACCOUNTS HELD IN JOINT TENANCY

It is advisable to **LEAVE ONE JOINT CHECKING ACCOUNT OPEN FOR AT LEAST TWO YEARS,** in case post-death checks/payments are slow to arrive.

Institution	Account Type & Number	Value	Ownership	Contact Information	Username	Password

BANK ACCOUNTS HELD IN MY NAME ONLY

Institution	Account Type & Number	Value	Ownership	Contact Information	Username	Password

INVESTMENT ACCOUNTS

INVESTMENT ACCOUNTS HELD IN SPOUSE'S NAME ONLY

Reminder: These funds will be available to you only after official release of the funds following proper notification of death by authorized executor or trustee.

Institution	Account Type & Number	Value	Ownership	Contact Information	Username	Password

INVESTMENT ACCOUNTS HELD IN JOINT TENANCY

Institution	Account Type & Number	Value	Ownership	Contact Information	Username	Password

INVESTMENT ACCOUNTS HELD IN MY NAME ONLY

Institution	Account Type & Number	Value	Ownership	Contact Information	Username	Password

QUALIFIED RETIREMENT PLANS

These include Traditional and Roth IRAs, 401K, 403B, SEPS, SIMPLES, etc. Determine your options for moving the remaining funds in your spouse's accounts. These accounts may be handled through your spouse's employer, brokers, or through financial advisors. **You want to handle these transfers in a way that minimizes tax consequences.** Have your options and the tax consequences of those options explained to you. Then meet with your financial advisor and tax accountant to determine how to move these funds. Be careful in naming and transferring these accounts. **Always** verify that the paperwork/transfer of funds was completed as you intended.

RETIREMENT ACCOUNTS HELD IN SPOUSE'S NAME ONLY

Account	Type	Policy Number	Value	Contact Name	Contact Number	Beneficiary

RETIREMENT ACCOUNTS HELD IN MY NAME ONLY

Account	Type	Policy Number	Value	Contact Name	Contact Number	Beneficiary

INSURANCE POLICIES I INTEND TO KEEP

Include any remaining insurance policies that you have not yet activated.

Company	Policy Number	Beneficiaries	Cash Surrender Value	Premium Amount	Contact Number	Coverage Changes

NON-FINANCIAL ASSETS

These can include items such a cars, boats, RVs, homes, coins, guns, jewelry, and collectibles that your spouse had. Decide whether you intend to keep each of these assets, sell them, or donate them.

Asset	Current Value	Amount Owed	Owner	Keep, sell, or donate?

WHO ARE THE NEW BENEFICIARIES?

Review the beneficiaries of all assets that you have listed on pages 30-41 and are keeping, make sure that your spouse is no longer named as a beneficiary or owner, and name the new beneficiaries for each remaining asset. Beneficiaries can be named through the trust or will for most assets, but not all.

Talk with your lawyer to make sure that you are doing this correctly. If you name one beneficiary on the paperwork of the asset itself (e.g. life insurance policy) and a different beneficiary in your will or trust, the law will determine which beneficiary takes precedent. If no beneficiary is named, the law will determine who inherits and that beneficiary may not be to your wishes.

ACCOUNTS WHERE BENEFICIARIES NEED TO BE CHANGED

Asset	Old Primary Beneficiary	New Primary Beneficiary	Old Secondary Beneficiary	New Secondary Beneficiary	How Changed?	Date Completed

SUMMARY OF ASSETS AND COST BASIS

There is a term called *step-up in cost basis* that is applied to many of the deceased person's assets (house, stock, bonds, etc). *Cost basis* is the price of an asset for tax purposes. A step-up in *cost basis* is applied to property transferred at death. It is the fair market value of the asset at the time it is inherited, not when it was bought.

When the *cost basis* is increased, there will be less profit when the item is sold, resulting in less taxes being paid. Therefore, it is important to know what those *cost basis* values are and document how those values were determined. Summarize the key items in the following tables.

Check with your accountant to get the most up-to-date list of items for which you will need to determine the stepped-up *cost basis*. The asset inventory at the time of death is broken up into the next two tables – financial and non-financial assets. Use the remaining accounts from pages 30-41 plus page 43 to complete this table.

ASSET INVENTORY WITH COST BASIS - PART 1 – FINACIAL ASSETS

Asset	Institution	Account Number	Current Value	Cost Basis	Owner	Beneficiary

ASSET INVENTORY PART 2: NON-FINANCIAL ASSETS

Asset	Current Value	Cost Basis	Owner	Beneficiary

LIABILITIES: MORTGAGES, LOANS, AND NOTES
(including home mortgages, equity lines of credit, student loans, and notes payable)

These are the outstanding debts that remain after enacting all the credit life insurance policies and after any other debt forgiveness and priority payment of spouse's debts when assets were insufficient to cover all of spouse's debts. This table should include the information from page 57 plus any liabilities held in your name that you haven't already paid off.

Mortgages Loans, & Notes	Person/Company Being Paid	Amount	Payment Terms	Remaining Balance	Amount in Arrears	Final Payment Due
TOTAL UNPAID BALANCES						

How will you handle the disposition of items you do not need that still carry debt? Will you sell the product and use the proceeds to pay off or pay down the debt?

DEBTS AND BILLS: MAINTAIN, REDUCE, OR ELIMINATE?

Up to now we have been focused on where your money will be coming from, how much that will be, and other funds you have available. Now we turn to the bills that are coming in. Yes, they just keep coming!

First, list all the debts and bills that your household has – separated into the appropriate table of whether owned by you, your spouse, or jointly. Although the primary purpose is to settle your spouse's estate, by including the bills that you yourself currently pay, you will have a complete picture of your household income and expenses when you are finished with settling the estate. Indicate what company is being paid, how much, how often, and through which account.

Place the information in the correct table based on who owns the debt. Find both the bills that are automatically paid electronically and those for which checks are written. The last monthly checking account or credit card statements will be a good source, but also remember that there are bills that are paid only quarterly or annually.

CURRENT DEBTS AND BILLS HELD IN SPOUSE'S NAME

Before you pay any of your spouse's debts, first determine whether there are any credit life insurance policies available to pay part or all of these bills. See page 56.

Institution	Account Number	Service/ Product Paid For	Paid Through Account Name & Number	Amount Due	Date Due

Institution	Account Number	Service/ Product Paid For	Paid Through Account Name & Number	Amount Due	Date Due

CURRENT DEBTS AND BILLS HELD IN JOINT TENANCY

Institution	Account Number	Service/ Product Paid For	Paid Through Account Name & Number	Amount Due	Date Due

Institution	Account Number	Service/ Product Paid For	Paid Through Account Name & Number	Amount Due	Date Due

CURRENT DEBTS AND BILLS HELD IN MY NAME

Institution	Account Number	Service/ Product Paid For	Paid Through Account Name & Number	Amount Due	Date Due

Institution	Account Number	Service/ Product Paid For	Paid Through Account Name & Number	Amount Due	Date Due

ENACTING CREDIT LIFE INSURANCE POLICIES

If a person dies with a balance owed on some debts, an insurance policy on that account may activate, paying the balance owed at the time of the deceased's death. These policies are sometimes found on credit cards, mortgages, travel insurance, auto insurance, homeowner insurance, or federal student loans. Contact the institutions where the debts are held and they will let you know how much, if any, debt forgiveness there is. You can also check your contract. These policies may help reduce your immediate expenses.

You can simultaneously cancel any of the accounts you will no longer be using.

Institution	Contract Number	Contact Person	Phone Number	Amount Owed	Amount Forgiven

SPOUSE'S REMAINING LIABILITIES:

Not every debt that your spouse had at the time of death will be paid off by credit life insurance policies. List those debts that remain and then check with your lawyer to verify which of the remaining debts you are required to pay off and in what priority order. This includes any home mortgages, equity lines of credit, student loans, and notes payable.

Company to Be Paid	Service/Product	Account Number	Unpaid Balance	Average Monthly Payment	Payment Priority Order
TOTAL UNPAID BALANCES					

NOW WHAT BILLS CAN I CANCEL?

After **enacting all the available credit life insurance policies and then** meeting with your lawyer to determine which of your spouse's remaining debts are to be paid and in what order, you are now ready to figure out which bills to stop, which to reduce, and which to keep.

In the tables below list those bills that you intend to cancel, (typically, deceased spouse's gym membership, recreational activity memberships, social memberships, toll collections, print & online subscriptions, charitable organizations, periodicals, mobile devices, airline mileage accounts, other services) based on current ownership. This will make it easier for you to track your work.

Start first with the accounts to be cancelled immediately. This could save you some money. **You might be able to get a refund of any unused portion of a prepaid fee, so don't forget to ask for that when you are cancelling a service.**

BILLS HELD IN SPOUSE'S NAME ONLY

Company Paid	Product / Service	Date Due	Paid Through Account	Amount	Phone # or Website address	Date Cancelled

BILLS HELD IN JOINT TENANCY

Company Paid	Product / Service	Date Due	Paid Through Account	Amount	Phone # or Website address	Date Cancelled

BILLS HELD IN MY NAME ONLY

Company Paid	Product / Service	Date Due	Paid Through Account	Amount	Phone # or Website address	Date Cancelled

BILLS I WANT TO REDUCE

In the following tables list those bills that you intend to continue, but at a reduced amount, in the appropriate ownership table. Some possible bills that you might want to reduce include cell phones, gym memberships, and cars.)

Determine from which account the reduced bills will be paid and make sure that the account has the correct names and authorizations on it. Once an institution is notified of the death of your spouse, the institution may require the passwords and security questions be reset.

BILLS HELD IN SPOUSE'S NAME ONLY

Company Being Paid	Old Amount	Paid Through Account	Company Contact	Date 1st Reduced Bill	New Amount	Owner Info Corrected?

BILLS HELD IN JOINT TENANCY

Company Being Paid	Old Amount	Paid Through Account	Company Contact	Date 1st Reduced Bill	New Amount	Owner Info Corrected?

BILLS HELD IN MY NAME ONLY

Company Being Paid	Old Amount	Paid Through Account	Company Contact	Date 1st Reduced Bill	New Amount	Owner Info Corrected?

EXPENSES I WANT TO KEEP
AT CURRENT LEVEL

Lastly, call the companies that you want to keep the same level of service. Determine from which account the bills will be paid and make sure that you have transferred the account into your name. Passwords and security questions may need to be reset.

BILLS HELD IN SPOUSE'S NAME ONLY

Company Being Paid	Amount	Date Due	Owner Info Changed?	Revised Account Information

BILLS HELD IN JOINT TENANCY

Company Being Paid	Amount	Date Due	Owner Info Changed?	Revised Account Information

BILLS HELD IN MY NAME ONLY

Company Being Paid	Amount	Date Due	Revised Account Information

NEW HOUSEHOLD MONTHLY EXPENSES SUMMARY

After you have eliminated the bills for services that you no longer need, reduced others to the level you now need, and changed ownership on the remaining accounts into your name, this table allows you to summarize all your remaining expenses on a monthly basis. Use the information in the tables on pages 63-69 to complete the table below.

Not all bills will be paid on a monthly basis. For those that are paid on a quarterly basis, if you want to budget an amount each month, divide the amount that you pay each quarter by 3, then add that amount to this table. For those that are paid on an annual basis, if you want to budget an amount each month, divide the amount that you pay each year by 12, then add that amount to this table. By budgeting monthly for every quarter or annual bill, there will be less worry about how you will pay the bill when it comes due.

Institution	Account Number	Service/Product	Contact Information	Monthly Amount

Institution	Account Number	Service/Product	Contact Information	Monthly Amount

SOCIAL MEDIA / OTHER ONLINE ACCOUNTS

Many wills and trusts now give executors and trustees the authority to handle the disposition of these accounts. Unsubscribe/cancel your spouse's personal accounts to minimize the risk of hacking your accounts. Always check with your lawyer before cancelling any business accounts. Your spouse's password list can be an excellent source of which accounts need to be addressed.

Some accounts will stop access the minute you notify them of your spouse's death. If you have to reset passwords, sometimes that can't be done until you present a copy of the death certificate.

Account Name	Username	Password	Keep or Cancel?	Date Account Cancelled

Account Name	User Name	Password	Keep or Cancel?	Date Account Cancelled

SUMMARY SECTION

Congratulations! You have now completed settling the estate. This next section is a place for you to summarize new household budget and to calculate your current household net worth.

NET WORTH SUMMARY

Use the information in the assets and liabilities tables found on pages 45-47, respectively, to complete the table below.

ASSET TYPE	VALUE	LIABILITY TYPE	UNPAID BALANCE
Bank Accounts		Mortgages	
Investment Accounts		Unpaid Credit Card Balances	
Retirement Accounts		Student Loans	
Real Estate		Other Debt	
Other		TOTAL	
TOTAL			

Net Worth = Total Assets ($_____) minus Total Debts ($_____) = $_____

MONTHLY BUDGET

Use the information found on pages 27 and 70-71, respectively, to complete the table below.

INCOME SOURCES	AMOUNT	EXPENSE SOURCES	AMOUNT
Salary		Housing	
Pension		Food	
Insurance		Utilities	
Rental Income		Entertainment	
Investment Income		Child care	
Other		Schooling	
TOTAL		Clothing & Grooming	
		Medical	
		Pets	
		Charitable	
		Vehicles & Transportation	
		Other	
		TOTAL	

Monthly budget = monthly income _____minus monthly expenses_____= $_____. If the number is positive, congratulations! You have a surplus of funds each month. If the number is negative, you will need to address where you can cut back on expenses to bring your income and outgo into balance. The goal is to have your income greater than your expenses. This may take several reworks of your expenses to get to that point but keep at it. You will be happy that you did. If you can't get your income to be greater than your expenses, you will need to start using money from savings accounts or other assets to balance your budget.

RECOMMENDED READING

Alpert, Susan C. *Driving Solo: Dealing With Grief and the Business of Financial Survival*. United States: Barana Books, 2013. Print.

Byrne, Anna E. *A Widow's Guide: Your Legal and Financial Guide to Surviving the First Year*. United States North Charleston, SC: Flower Press Publishing, CreateSpace Independent Publishing Platform, 2016. Print

Calligaro, Julie A. *The Widow's Resource: How to Solve the Financial and Legal Problems That Occur Within the First Six to Nine Months of Your Husband's Death*. Grosse Ile, Mich: Women's Source Books Publishers, 1997. Print

Colgan, Mark R. *Details After Death: Navigating the Logistics After a Loved One Dies*. Pittsford, NY: Plan Your Legacy, 2017. Print.

Dunnan, Nancy. *The Widow's Financial Survival Guide: Handling Money Matters on Your Own*. New York: Perigee, 2003. Print.

Handke, Bridget. *Finances for One: A New Widow's Guide to Managing Money.* 2014. Print.

Hanks, Liza W., and Carol Zolla. *The Trustee's Legal Companion*. Berkeley, CA: Nolo, 2019. Print.

Hoffman, David G. *The Essential Executor's Handbook.* Wayne, NJ: Career Press, 2016. Print.

Houck, Maurcia D. *Living Life After Divorce & Widowhood, Financial Planning, Skills, and Strategies for When the Unthinkable Happens*. Ocala, Fla: Atlantic Pub. Group, 2010. Print.

Munro, Margaret A., and Kathryn A. Murphy. *Estate & Trust Administration*. Hoboken, NJ: For Dummies, a Wiley Brand John Wiley & Sons, Inc, 2019. Print

Phillips, Shane. *First Steps: A Comprehensive Guide to Financial Matters After a Death*. Castle Rock, Colorado: First Step Solutions, LLC, 2013. Print.

Randolph, Mary. *The Executor's Guide: Settling a Loved One's Estate or Trust*. Berkeley, California: Nolo, 2018. Print

Rust, David, and Shane Moore. *Single – Not by Choice: Emotional and Financial Guidance for Women After the Loss of Their Spouse*. The Sudden Wealth Center. 2018. Print.

www.ingramcontent.com/pod-product-compliance
Lightning Source LLC
Chambersburg PA
CBHW060530010526
44110CB00052B/2548